Sounds Good!

DISCOVER 50 INSTRUMENTS

Text and illustrations
Ole Könnecke

Music
Hans Könnecke

Translated by
Melody Shaw

GECKO PRESS

50 INSTRUMENTS

We could have chosen 40 or 60 or 600, of course; there's no shortage of musical instruments. But 50 is a fine number, and we have all the most popular instruments, plus a few less well known ones. Here they are, in order of appearance.

DRUM KIT	DULCIMER	MANDOLIN	ORGAN
GUITAR	STEELPAN	RECORDER	PIANO
PAN PIPES	FLUTE	BASSOON	CONCERTINA
SITAR	THEREMIN	KAZOO	ELECTRIC GUITAR
BONGOS	CLARINET	DIDGERIDOO	DOUBLE BASS
CONGAS	GLOCKENSPIEL	JAW HARP	BASS GUITAR
CASTANETS	TUBA	VIBRAPHONE	ELECTRIC PIANO
VIOLIN	TRUMPET	LUTE	COMPUTER
VIOLA	HORN	LUR	TRIANGLE
KALIMBA	HARMONICA	TROMBONE	BASS VOICE
CELLO	BANJO	ACCORDION	TENOR VOICE
HARP	OBOE	SAXOPHONE	ALTO VOICE
BAGPIPES	COR ANGLAIS	UKULELE	SOPRANO VOICE

Music experts will notice that we haven't divided the instruments into their usual families (woodwind, brass, strings, percussion). We learned music unsystematically. This book is about playing, about discovery. Why only listen to pop, when there's so much great classical music out there? Why stick to jazz, when there are so many fantastic country songs?

Ole wrote the words and drew the pictures. While musical instruments are lovely to look at, they are even lovelier to listen to. That's why Hans composed a musical piece for each instrument. Scan the QR code on each page with a smartphone, and the track will pop up (provided your phone is connected to the internet). Simple. You can hear all the instruments playing together by scanning the QR code on the facing page and at the back of the book.

Ole & Hans

P.S. We just counted again. There are 52 instruments.
But that's okay, right?

DRUM KIT

Of course, nobody knows for certain what the first musical instruments were. But they're almost certain to have been percussive. Clapping hands, stamping feet, hitting a tree trunk with a branch—that's where drumming probably started. Now we have drum kits: an assortment of drums and cymbals. Jazz, rock or pop without drums? Unthinkable.

GUITAR

A guitar has six strings, usually made of nylon, sometimes steel. Originally, most instrument strings were made from animal intestines. Not so much these days. Musicians have written highly virtuoso solo pieces for the guitar, but even if 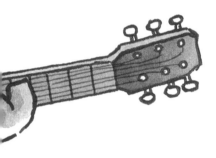 you can only play two or three chords, you can have a lot of fun with a guitar.

MUSIC

PAN PIPES

Pan pipes are one of the oldest musical instruments. They've been around since the Stone Age in Europe, and they're found all over the world. No wonder, because the principle is simple, and so is the construction. Tie together hollow tubes of different lengths. That's it. Then blow across the top of each tube, and those are your notes. You can try this technique with a bottle.

MUSIC

SITAR

The sitar comes from India and is a
member of the long-necked lute family.
It has quite a number of strings: some
for the melody and others that resonate in
harmony. A sitar has metal frets, which you can
slide along the neck to change the tuning. We wouldn't
exactly say the sitar is an easy instrument to learn.

MUSIC

BONGOS, CONGAS AND CASTANETS

Three different rhythm instruments that sound great together. Bongos (the two small drums) and congas (the two larger ones) both originate from Cuba. Although we associate castanets with Spain, they probably weren't invented there. Traditional castanets are held in the hand and played with the fingers. The others are called handle castanets.

MUSIC

VIOLIN

In some ways, the violin is the ideal instrument. It's small and easy to carry. You can play it loud enough to be heard in the back row of a concert hall or softly enough not to disturb the people next door. But there's a catch: it takes a huge amount of practice to be a really good violinist. (Or you could strike a bargain with the devil—something many violin players have been accused of down the ages, from virtuoso classical violinists to wandering musicians who drove village festivalgoers to a frenzy with their wild music.)

MUSIC

VIOLA

It's not easy to tell the violin and viola apart. Both have the same shape and four strings played with a bow. They also appeared at the same time, around 1600, in northern Italy. (Of course, they had plenty of ancestors. Bowed stringed instruments have existed for thousands of years, pretty much everywhere in the world.) The viola is slightly larger than the violin and therefore more difficult to play because the strings are further apart and harder to hold down. The upshot: fewer solo pieces have been composed for the viola. Poor viola. It has such a beautiful tone—somewhat lower than the violin, but indispensable in a string quartet, bridging the gap between the higher violin and the even deeper cello.

MUSIC

KALIMBA

An old African instrument, also called the mbira.
Tines (or keys) are attached to a soundboard
(a kind of box). The tines were originally made
from tough palm leaves (or more precisely, stalks)
and later from metal. The tines are of different
lengths, which produce different notes.

MUSIC

CELLO

You can see at a glance that the cello (or violoncello, its full name) is related to the violin and viola. Same shape, same wood, and with four strings that are bowed or plucked. The cello is so big, you have to stand it on the ground to play it. Well, not directly on the ground: the cello rests on a spike called an endpin. That way, the sound doesn't get muted, and the cello stays dry—just in case you feel like playing it outdoors. The cello has a deep, rich and expressive sound, and many solo passages have been written for it, though it is also a key instrument in a string quartet.

MUSIC

HARP

Imagine this: many thousands of years ago, someone shooting an arrow from a bow noticed that the bowstring sounded a note. Then if they pressed the tip of the bow against a hollow tree and plucked the string, the note became louder and fuller and lovelier. Then if they attached a second string, they got two different notes. And then a third string…and a fourth…and that's how the harp was invented. Maybe.

MUSIC

BAGPIPES

As you might guess from the name, bagpipes are a leather bag with several pipes poking out. One pipe is for blowing air into the bag. When you squeeze the bag, air escapes through the other pipes. One of them has holes like a recorder, for playing the melody. (Want to learn a new word? It's called the chanter.) The other pipes with no holes sound one low note each and are called the drones. Like the bees, they hum in the background.

MUSIC

DULCIMER

The dulcimer (or Appalachian dulcimer) is a simple stringed instrument that was played by European immigrants in North America. It looks a little like a zither with a bit of violin. It was probably developed from the instruments people brought with them from Europe. It has only three strings. In the past, it was played with a feather; today, players tend to use a plastic plectrum (also called a pick).

MUSIC

STEELPAN

Around 1930, someone in Trinidad had the idea of using an old oil drum as a musical instrument. They hammered domes into the lid so different parts of it produced different notes, cut off the bottom part of the drum, and voilà! The more of the drum that's cut off, the higher the notes. Now all you need are some wooden sticks to play it.

MUSIC

FLUTE

In the past, flutes were made of wood. They looked
pretty but sounded quiet. Now they're made of metal,
they look at least as pretty, and you can play them
REALLY LOUD. If you want to. Because the
flute is quite long, it has keys, not fingerholes—
sixteen altogether. The flute is a wind instrument,
but half of the air is blown over the top and away
(like the pan pipes).

MUSIC

THEREMIN

A hundred years ago, Russian physicist Leon Theremin invented the first instrument to be played by NOT touching it. He packed two generators into a box with two antennae poking out (one straight up, one curving sideways). Somehow (it involves electromagnetism), the instrument produces a sound. If you hold your hand close to one of the antennae and wave it gently, the pitch changes. At first, the instrument was called the etherophone, but Theremin decided "theremin" was a much better name. For a time, the theremin was popular for making spooky music in horror and sci-fi films.

MUSIC

CLARINET

The clarinet works like this: fasten a small, rectangular piece of reed to a mouthpiece, attach the mouthpiece to the instrument and now, if you blow into it juuust right, it creates a note. The clarinet has been around since 1700, but the idea of using a reed is ancient. The great thing about the clarinet is its wide range, thanks to oodles of keys that regulate the pitch. And if you use a special blowing technique called overblowing—more breath pressure to create a higher note—you can take it from deep, warm aahs to high, trumpet-like toots. But you have to be a pretty skilled player to do that.

MUSIC

GLOCKENSPIEL

A few metal bars, a wooden sound box—there's not much to the glockenspiel. But enough to play simple melodies with small mallets. Larger glockenspiels with more sophisticated features are used in orchestras. The xylophone is an instrument that looks and sounds similar, but its bars are made from wood.

MUSIC

TUBA

If there's such a thing as a laid-back brass instrument,
it's the tuba. It is (usually) played sitting down. It has
a comfy shape and a pleasant sound. Only its very
deepest notes are able to sound threatening. If you
could uncoil a standard tuba, it would be three or four
times taller than you. But you can find extra-large
tubas that would stretch out to the length of eight
times your height.

MUSIC

TRUMPET

Trumpets have been around for a long, long time. Of all the brass instruments, trumpets blare out the loudest blast. No wonder they've often been used to sound the alarm. For hundreds of years, people could only play harmonic notes on the trumpet (tense your lips for a high note; tense your lips less for a lower note). You can't get very many notes this way. Then someone invented valves, and suddenly almost anything was possible. Pressing the valves opens and closes different parts of the tubing to change its length, producing different notes.

MUSIC

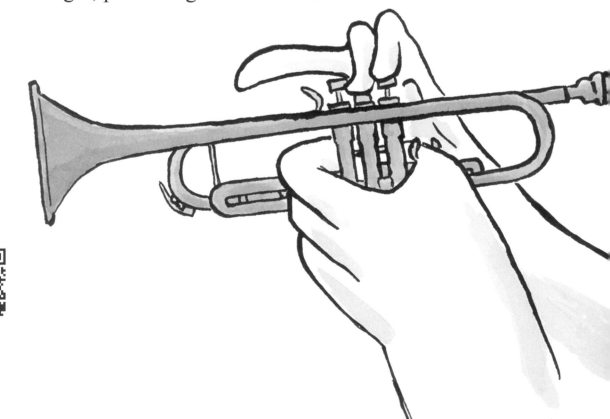

HORN

As with the trumpet, valves were added to the horn quite late in its history—around 1820. The horn is also commonly known as the French horn. Or the German horn. It's had quite an international career. The horn has a soft, warm tone. When composers in the Romantic era wanted to conjure up a dreamy forest atmosphere (and they often did), the horn was the instrument of choice.

HARMONICA

You hold a harmonica to your lips. Breathe in through the harmonica, and it plays a note. Breathe out through the harmonica, and it plays a different note—even though you haven't moved the instrument. If the harmonica didn't have two notes in the same position, it would have to be twice as long—and then it wouldn't fit in your pocket.

MUSIC

BANJO

This African instrument originated in North America. Africans kept as slaves built a plucked instrument reminiscent of those in their homelands. They took a round drum (with a skin on one side only), attached a long neck and added strings: job done. The banjo evolved over the years, and now it's quite similar to the guitar. Before the electric guitar was invented, the banjo played an important role in early jazz bands. Nowadays, it's mostly used in American bluegrass, a type of country music.

MUSIC

OBOE

The oboe is one of the oldest instruments to ever be invented. Even the ancient Egyptians had oboes, although they didn't look much like the one in this picture. What the ancient and modern oboe have in common is the double reed. Using reeds in musical instruments developed from the discovery that blowing through a reed produces a fantastic squawking noise. The earliest double reeds were made by cutting a reed into two sections, holding the rounded edges together, putting these into a larger, hollow reed, then blowing down on it. The way the reeds vibrate produces different notes. The oboe in its modern form has only been around since the 19th century, but it still uses two "reeds" (these days made from cane).

MUSIC

COR ANGLAIS

The cor anglais, or English horn, is just a slightly larger oboe with a comedy bulge at the bottom end. Like the oboe, the cor anglais got its keys in the 19th century, making it easier to play and extending its tonal range. By the way, the name itself has nothing to do with England. It came about because the original word could mean both "angelic" and "English." The instrument was actually named for the angelic beauty of its music.

MUSIC

MANDOLIN

Mandolins vary in appearance. Some have a rounded body, like a lute. Modern mandolins can be flat, like a guitar. But all mandolins have four double strings—eight in total. They are tuned to the same notes as a violin. People who can already play the violin shouldn't have too much trouble with the mandolin. There are orchestras made up entirely of mandolins, but it's just as much fun to play solo.

MUSIC

RECORDER

The oldest surviving example of a recorder dates from the 14th century, but we're sure it's been around much longer. Back then, the recorder was carved from a single piece of wood. Since the Baroque period, it's been made of several pieces. This makes it easier to carry around and means you can adjust its length slightly to change the pitch—in case you ever need to tune it to other instruments.

MUSIC

BASSOON

Like the oboe and the cor anglais, the bassoon is a double-reeded wind instrument. The biggest of the lot.

You can't tell by looking, but inside, the bassoon doubles back on itself, which means if you stretched out its insides, it would be longer than a giraffe's neck.

That extra length means it can play deep notes.

The keys on a bassoon are pretty complicated.

MUSIC

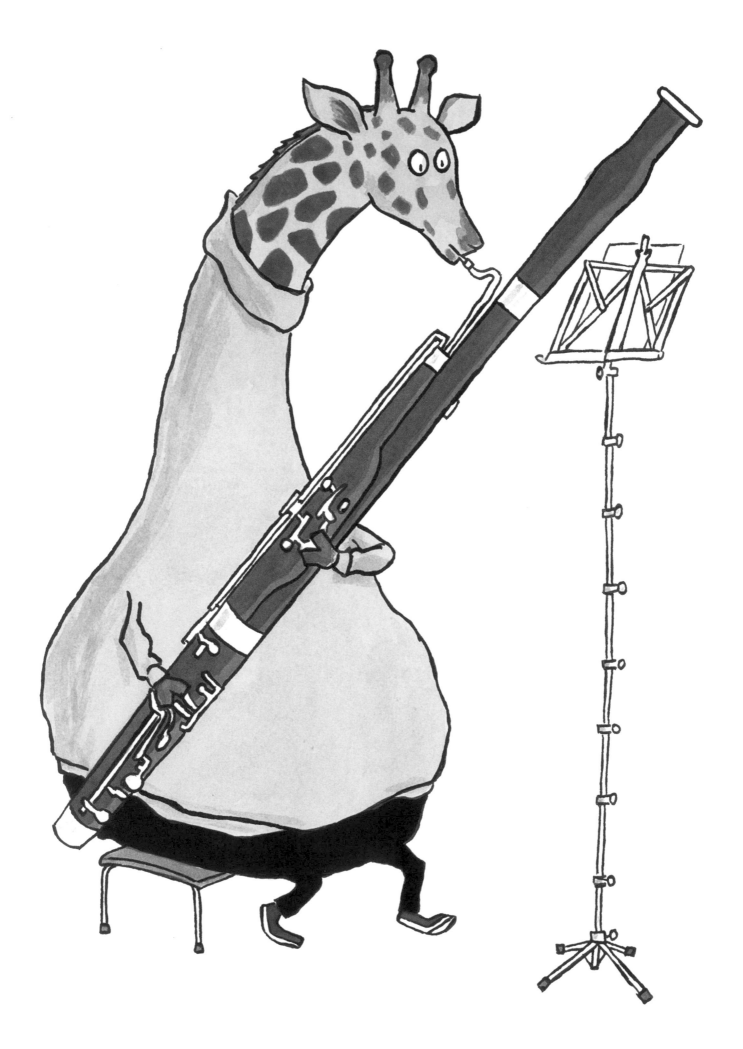

KAZOO

One of the few instruments where you can go from beginner to virtuoso in 30 seconds. The kazoo is a pipe, usually plastic or metal, open at both ends. It has a membrane across another opening on top. If you sing into it with a high-pitched voice, the membrane vibrates, creating a distinctive, slightly nasal sound.

MUSIC

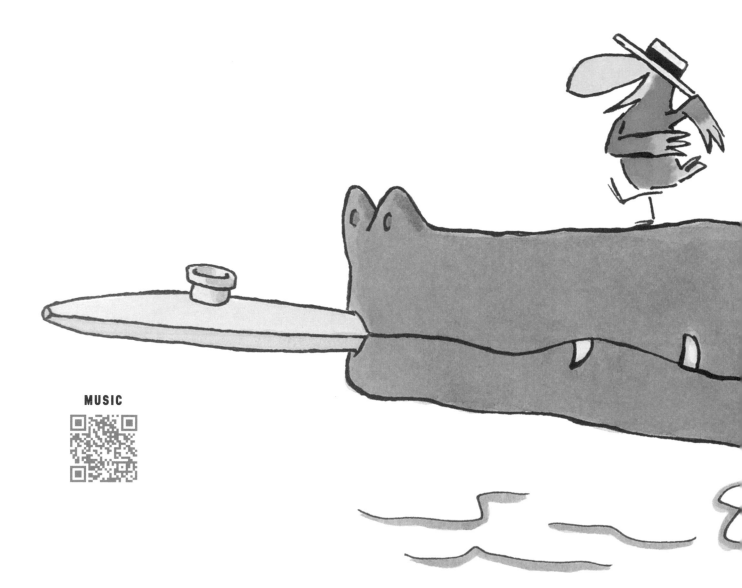

(You've probably taken 30 seconds to read this page.

In that time, you could've learned to play the kazoo.)

DIDGERIDOO

The didgeridoo is a long, hollow branch. You press your lips to the narrower end and blow, letting your lips vibrate a little. This produces a deep drone. At the same time, you can sing into the didgeridoo, or trill with your tongue, or change the shape of your mouth. This creates overtones over the drone.

MUSIC

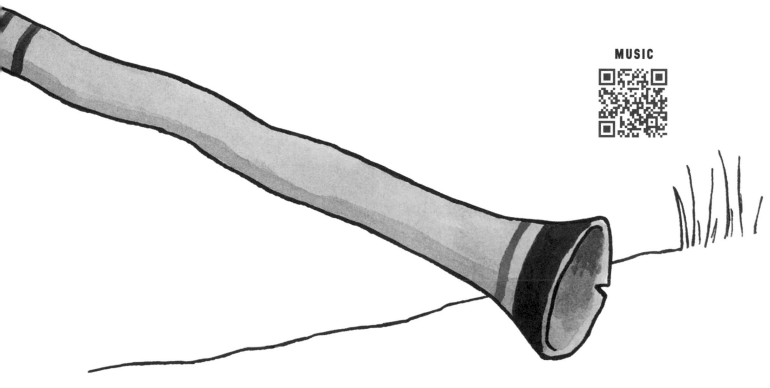

JAW HARP

On this funny little instrument you can play simple melodies—with a bit of practice. You press the jaw harp against your teeth and pluck at the curved metal tongue. Get it just right, and it will sound a note that you can alter by opening or closing your mouth.

MUSIC

VIBRAPHONE

The vibraphone is a relatively modern instrument, developed in the USA in the early decades of the 20th century. Its special feature: an electrical device that gives each note a vibrato sound (a regular slight rise and fall in pitch). Like most instruments less than 200 years old, the vibraphone has not found a permanent place in the symphony orchestra. But it's very much at home in a jazz band.

LUTE

For a time, the lute was enormously popular in Europe. And no wonder: people could play beautiful melodies on it or accompany a singer. Five hundred years ago, the lute was the celebrity of the instrument world. Then along came the guitar and the piano and suddenly the lute was so last year. (But it's still a beautiful instrument.)

MUSIC

LUR

Long ago (very long ago), people made musical instruments from whatever was at hand. Hollow tree trunks made good drums. A cow's horn (or back then, more likely from its great-great-grandma, the aurochs) could be used as a kind of trumpet. Or mammoth tusks! Make a hole in the tip, purse your lips, and blow—what a glorious, deep honk! Then one day there were no more mammoths, but luckily the Bronze Age had dawned. Now people could make a lur from metal based on the shape of the tusk. A few dating from that time still exist. Is this how it happened? We don't know for sure, but the lur does look suspiciously like a mammoth tusk…

MUSIC

TROMBONE

The trombone has been around for a long time (it was originally called a sackbut) but has only had a slider since the 15th century. The slider lets you extend the trombone's length to change its pitch. The further you push it, the deeper the note. The first time a trombone was played in public was at the wedding of Charles the Bold, Duke of Burgundy, and Princess Margaret of England. During the banquet, the musicians had to dress as animals. The trombonist was dressed as a goat.

MUSIC

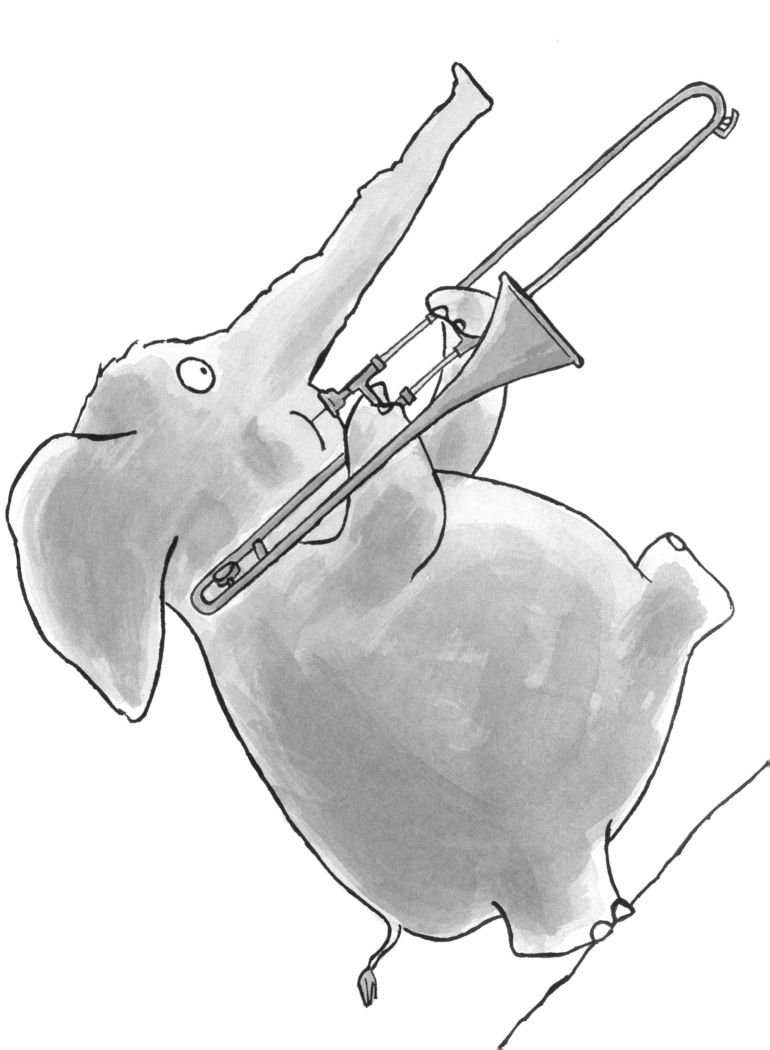

ACCORDION

When you play several notes at the same time that sound good together, that's a chord. And what better instrument to play a chord on than an accordion? Other instruments play chords, such as the piano or guitar, but the clever thing about the accordion is that you only press a single button to play a whole chord. The chord buttons are on the left. On the right is a keyboard—called a manual—for playing individual notes. So you play the melody with the right hand, and the accompaniment with the left.

SAXOPHONE

The saxophone was invented in the 1840s by Belgian instrument maker Adolphe Sax. It has a similar mouthpiece to the clarinet but can be played much louder. The saxophone has never been a big star of the symphony orchestra, but 70 years after it was invented, it became *the* jazz instrument. Sometimes you just need to wait for your moment in the spotlight. What a shame Adolphe Sax never lived to see it: he died in 1894 in Paris.

MUSIC

UKULELE

A hundred years ago, the ukulele was the height of fashion. This small guitar-like instrument from Hawai'i was hugely popular in North America. It was easy to play (having only four strings), endearingly funny and, of course, good to sing along to. Every few years, the ukulele makes a massive comeback, then sinks into obscurity to wait for the next surefire comeback.

MUSIC

ORGAN

The organ is loud, majestic and awe-inspiring. For centuries it has been used for sacred music. No one would ever dream of playing secular (normal, everyday) music on it. NEVER, d'you hear?

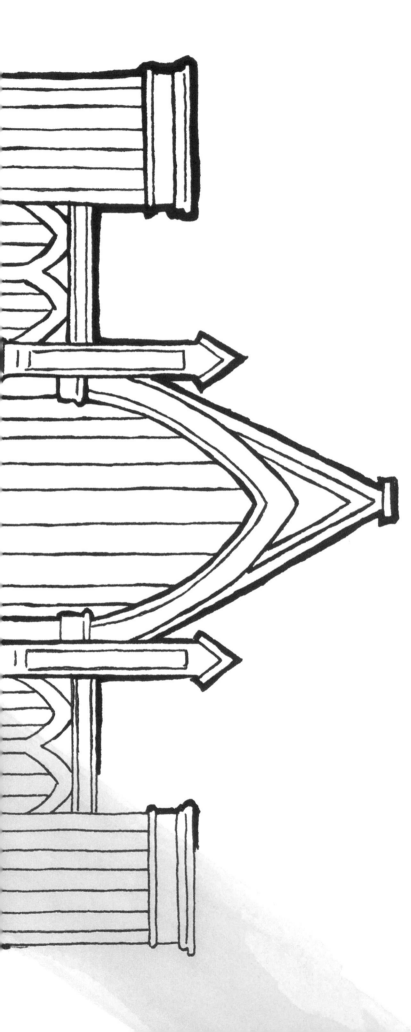

PIANO

Perhaps the best-loved instrument in the world. At least, one of the three best-loved. The guitar is certainly another. We'll leave the third place open; we don't want any trouble from the other instruments. With its impressive total of 88 keys, the piano takes a few years to learn to play. Many composers use the piano to develop and try out their pieces. That works even if they can't play very well. Renowned composer Irving Berlin could only play the piano in one key (F sharp major), and even then, only just. Regardless, he composed some of the most famous songs of the last century at the piano.

CONCERTINA

The concertina is a relatively simple instrument. Each of its buttons plays a single note. Operate the bellows, press the button, and inside the instrument the air pressure makes a small metal prong vibrate. Out comes the note! The concertina doesn't have many buttons, or notes, but enough to play some catchy melodies. What's more, the concertina is one of the very, very few hexagonal instruments. Which is pretty cool.

MUSIC

ELECTRIC GUITAR

The guitar is a fantastic instrument, but not especially loud. That changed in the early 1930s when the electric guitar was invented. Electric in the sense that the sound of a regular guitar was electrically amplified and played through a speaker. At a stroke—or a twang—the banjo was old hat for jazz bands. The guitar was simply more versatile. Soon people were making electric guitars without a resonant sound board; they only functioned with an amplifier. Electric guitars are the ultimate in cool—there's nothing like them.

MUSIC

DOUBLE BASS

The largest of the stringed instruments. Without the double bass, a symphony orchestra would sound a bit thin. The double bass is usually played with a bow, unless you're a jazz musician. Then you'd almost certainly pluck the strings. Together with the drums (or alone if there's no drummer), the double bass sets the rhythm. It doesn't often get to play a solo, so when it does, give it an extra-large round of applause, okay?

MUSIC

BASS GUITAR

The electric bass guitar was developed around the same time as the electric guitar. It just took a little longer to gain the same level of popularity. Even the early rock'n'roll bands of the 1950s preferred the

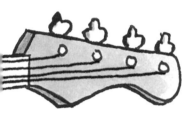

double bass. But since the 1960s, no band has had a chance of hitting the big time without a bass guitar. When four people form a band, if one of them plays drums and three play guitar, one has to give up guitar and take up bass guitar. Whether they want to or not— that's the way it is.

MUSIC

ELECTRIC PIANO

For a few years, the electric piano was the coolest musical instrument out there. You played it like a normal piano, but it sounded different. Electric. More modern. It started in the 1950s, carried on through the 1960s, then suddenly it was over. Lighter, more versatile electronic keyboards appeared. And then came the computer.

MUSIC

COMPUTER

You can play a computer like an instrument—
or a thousand instruments. You can create an
infinite number of artificial tones. You can record
actual instruments then completely alter their
sounds. You can tinker with music on a computer
even if you don't play a single instrument.
It's fascinating. And awesome.

MUSIC

TRIANGLE

Tllinnnng! Who would have thought such an

angular instrument could produce such a

beautiful sound? But lovely as it is, that

single note is all the triangle can play.

If you want different triangle notes,

you need different-sized triangles.

(But you can use the same beater

to play them.)

MUSIC

BASS VOICE

Is the voice a musical instrument? Absolutely!
If you know how, you can create the most
beautiful music with it. The human voice is
categorized into four vocal pitches. Bass is the
deepest. In operas, the bass is the preferred voice
for the villain, or the father, or occasionally for
comic roles. Very, very rarely is the bass allowed
to sing the part of the dashing hero. (Then again,
perhaps they wouldn't want to.)

MUSIC

TENOR VOICE

A tenor has no problem accepting the role of hero.
At least, if they're a heldentenor—literally, "heroic
tenor." There's also the lyric tenor, who has a
slightly softer and higher voice. Perfect for ballads
and soulful songs. The heldentenor, on the other
hand, with a more powerful voice, is well suited to
belting out operatic arias onstage. Whichever style,
"tenor" describes a higher vocal range for men
(and sometimes the deepest range for women).

MUSIC

ALTO VOICE

The deep singing voice of a woman (and sometimes a high man's voice). In opera, alto voices play a similar role to the bass: the main part is usually sung by someone else, but without the alto's dulcet tones, something would be missing.

MUSIC

SOPRANO VOICE

The highest singing voice. It takes years of practice to sing the soprano notes exactly right. Then even more years to sing them so they don't sound cold and lifeless, but warm and vibrant.

MUSIC

This edition first published in 2024 by Gecko Press
PO Box 9335, Wellington 6141, Aotearoa New Zealand
office@geckopress.com

English-language edition © Gecko Press Ltd 2024
Translation © Melody Shaw 2024

© 2022 Carl Hanser Verlag GmbH & Co. KG, München

Distributed in the United States and Canada
by Lerner Publishing Group, lernerbooks.com

Distributed in the United Kingdom and Ireland
by Bounce Sales and Marketing, bouncemarketing.co.uk

Distributed in Australia and New Zealand
by Walker Books Australia, walkerbooks.com.au

Gecko Press aims to publish with a low environmental
impact. Our books are printed using vegetable inks on
FSC-certified paper from sustainably managed forests.
We produce books of high quality with sewn bindings
and beautiful paper—made to be read over and over.

The translation of this work was supported by a grant
from the Goethe Institut

Original language: German
Edited by Penelope Todd
Cover design and typesetting by Spencer Levine

Printed in China by Everbest Printing Co. Ltd, an accredited
ISO 14001 & FSC-certified printer

ISBN hardback: 9781776575558

For more curiously good books, visit geckopress.com

MUSICIANS AND SINGERS

ALEXANDER VIČAR mandolin

ARABELLA PURUCKER clarinet, pan pipes and didgeridoo

DAVID FRANZEN bass voice

EGE ATESLIOGLU violin

EVA KRISTL oboe and cor anglais

FABIOLA WÖRTER alto voice and kazoo

HENRIKE LEGNER soprano voice

INES SOLTWEDEL violin

JONAS HÄUSLER tenor voice

JONAS HINTERMAIER bassoon

KORBINIAN BAUER drum kit

LUCIE KRYSATIS horn

LUKAS STIPAR trombone and lur

MARIA DIMITROVA accordion and concertina

MARIA ZWERSCHKE flute and recorder

MÁTÉ FRANK tuba

MICHEL SPEYER trumpet

NILS WRASSE saxophone

SARAH LUISA ZRENNER viola

SUSI LOTTER double bass and bass guitar

THERESA STRASSER cello

HANS KÖNNECKE composition, recordings, production
and mastering, and all other instruments

MUSIC